W9-BNN-016

Property of
Kent School District

# the Living Ocean

# the Amazing Octopus

**Bobbie Kalman & Rebecca Sjonger**

Illustrations by Margaret Amy Reiach

🌲 Crabtree Publishing Company

www.crabtreebooks.com

# Created by Bobbie Kalman

Dedicated by Rebecca Sjonger
For Tim, my very favorite fellow

**Editor-in-Chief**
Bobbie Kalman

**Writing team**
Bobbie Kalman
Rebecca Sjonger

**Editorial director**
Niki Walker

**Editors**
John Crossingham
Kathryn Smithyman

**Copy editor**
Molly Aloian

**Art director**
Robert MacGregor

**Design**
Margaret Amy Reiach

**Production coordinator**
Heather Fitzpatrick

**Photo research**
Laura Hysert

**Consultant**
Patricia Loesche, Ph.D., Animal Behavior Program,
Department of Psychology, University of Washington

**Photographs**
Tom Stack & Associates: David B. Fleetham: front cover, pages 1 (bottom),
4, 18, 28; Ed Robinson: pages 12, 17 (bottom)
Jeff Rotman Photography: Jeff Rotman: pages 14, 22
Copyright © Brandon Cole/www.brandoncole.com: pages 16, 31 (bottom)
Seapics.com: © Doug Perrine: pages 8, 19, 20; © Marilyn Kazmers: page 9 (top);
© Bob Cranston: pages 9 (bottom), 21 (top); © Masa Ushioda: page 13;
© Mark Conlin: page 15 (top); © David B. Fleetham: page 21 (bottom)
Visuals Unlimited: Steven Norvich: page 17 (top); Science VU/NOAA, NMFS:
page 23 (top & middle); Brandon D. Cole: page 23 (bottom);
John Forsythe: pages 15 (bottom), 30; John S. Lough: page 31 (top)
Other images by Digital Stock and Digital Vision

**Illustrations**
All illustrations by Margaret Amy Reiach except the following:
Barbara Bedell: pages 24-25 (squid, shrimp, mysid shrimp, sponges,
shark, moray eel)
Katherine Kantor: page 24 (sea horse)

## Crabtree Publishing Company

www.crabtreebooks.com     1-800-387-7650

PMB 16A
350 Fifth Avenue
Suite 3308
New York, NY
10118

612 Welland Avenue
St. Catharines
Ontario
Canada
L2M 5V6

73 Lime Walk
Headington
Oxford
OX3 7AD
United Kingdom

Copyright © **2003 CRABTREE PUBLISHING COMPANY.** All rights
reserved. No part of this publication may be reproduced, stored in a
retrieval system or be transmitted in any form or by any means,
electronic, mechanical, photocopying, recording, or otherwise, without
the prior written permission of Crabtree Publishing Company.

**Cataloging-in-Publication Data**
Kalman, Bobbie
    The amazing octopus / Bobbie Kalman & Rebecca Sjonger.
      p. cm. — (The Living ocean series)
This book explores how these tentacled animals move through
water, how they hunt, how they use camouflage and other
protection measures, and why octopuses are important in
oceans around the world.
    ISBN 0-7787-1299-0 (RLB) — ISBN 0-7787-1321-0 (pbk.)
    1. Octopus—Juvenile literature. [1. Octopus.] I. Sjonger, Rebbeca.
II. Title. III. Series.
    QL430.3.O2K35 2003
    594'.56—dc21

                                                                2003004494
                                                                LC

#  Contents

# What is an octopus?

Octopuses are **mollusks**. Mollusks are soft-bodied **invertebrates**, or animals that do not have backbones. In fact, octopuses do not have any bones at all! There are thousands of **species**, or types, of mollusks, including many kinds of snails, clams, and slugs.

Most mollusks have hard shells around their bodies for protection, but octopuses do not. Octopuses are so well **adapted**, or suited to, surviving in the ocean that they have little need for this kind of armor. Some octopuses, however, have shells on the inside of their bodies.

4

## Classmates

Octopuses belong to a very old **class**, or group, of water-dwelling mollusks called **cephalopods**. Other cephalopods include squids, cuttlefish, and chambered nautiluses. Cephalopods have arms—and some have **tentacles**—that circle their mouths. Squids and cuttlefish have eight arms and two tentacles, whereas chambered nautiluses have up to 90 short arms. Octopuses have eight arms. The word "okta" means "eight" in Greek.

*The chambered nautilus is called a "living fossil" because its body has not changed in millions of years.*

*Arms and tentacles are not the same. Tentacles are usually much longer than arms. It is easy to tell squids and octopuses apart because squids have tentacles.*

*A cuttlefish hides its tentacles in a pouch beneath its eyes.*

## Ancient animals

The first cephalopods appeared in Earth's oceans around 500 million years ago—before there were fish! During this time, they were common sea creatures. The ancient cephalopods lived in shells. Today, only the chambered nautilus has an outer shell. Octopuses, squids, and cuttlefish either have shells inside their bodies, or they have no shells at all.

*Ammonites are ancestors of octopuses that disappeared from Earth along with the dinosaurs about 70 million years ago.*

# Spectacular species

There are at least 250 known species of octopuses, but scientists are discovering more species every year! These pages show just a few of the octopus species that make up the group *Octopoda*. Scientists divide this group into two subgroups: **cirrate** octopuses and **incirrate** octopuses. Members of each subgroup have similar bodies and live in similar **habitats**.

*Sunlight does not reach into deep ocean waters. The **bioluminescent** octopus has body parts that glow bright blue-green in deep, dark waters.*

## Finned and fuzzy

Members of the cirrate subgroup have **cirri**, or hairlike growths, on their arms. Cirrate octopuses also have fins and large **webs**, or flaps of skin, between their arms.

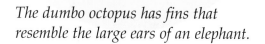

*The dumbo octopus has fins that resemble the large ears of an elephant.*

*The flapjack octopus resembles a pancake because of the wide webs connecting its arms.*

# Majority rules

Most octopuses belong to the incirrate subgroup. These octopuses have no cirri, and very few have fins or large webs.

*The giant Pacific octopus is the largest species of octopus. It grows up to 30 feet (9 m) in length and weighs up to 100 pounds (45 kg).*

*The common octopus is one of the best-known octopus species. It lives in warm ocean waters around the world.*

*The blue-ringed octopus is known for its deadly poison. Read more about this octopus on page 29.*

*The Californian octopus is the smallest type of octopus. It grows only to one inch (2.5 cm) in length.*

# Den dwellers

*Tropical seas and oceans, or those near the equator, are home to the greatest variety of octopuses.*

Octopuses live in all parts of the ocean. They can survive only in salt water. Incirrate octopuses are commonly found in shallow waters near shore, and cirrate octopuses usually live in deep waters far from shore. Small species tend to live in warm waters, whereas large species live in cold waters. Most octopuses are **bottom dwellers**, or animals that live on or close to the ocean floor.

## Home alone

Octopuses are **solitary** animals, which means they live alone. They spend a lot of time in their **dens**, or homes. Many octopuses make their dens in underwater caves or in spaces among coral reefs. Octopuses also live in sunken ships, empty seashells, and among piles of stones. Small octopuses have even made dens out of trash such as glass bottles and soda cans!

## Interior design

Octopuses occasionally rearrange their dens. Using their strong arms, they move rocks and stones to create better shelters. They also make the entrances to their dens smaller to attract less attention.

## Shells mark the spot

Some octopuses have two dens—one in an area where they can find plenty of food, and the other in a quiet spot. When an octopus has finished hunting, it carries its food to its quiet den, where it eats its meal. After eating shelled animals such as clams or crabs, it tosses the empty shells outside. **Middens**, or piles of discarded shells, help divers locate octopus dens. The octopus shown right has eaten many shelled animals!

## On the move

Scientists have little information about octopus **migration**, or long-distance travel from one region to another. Giant Pacific octopuses have a well-known migration path, however. In autumn, they move from **coastal** areas, or areas near shore, out to deeper waters. They return to coastal waters in spring.

# Octopus bodies

The soft, muscular body of an octopus is perfectly suited to surviving in the ocean. Although each species has its own distinct size and color, all octopuses have some body parts in common. Each octopus uses these parts in similar ways to swim, hunt, and protect itself.

*eyes*

*funnel tube*

*The **mantle** is a bag of skin and muscle that contains all the animal's organs.*

*In most species, the only hard body part is a beak, which looks like a parrot's beak. See page 23 for a close-up image.*

*mouth*

*webs*

## Breathing easily

An octopus breathes with **gills** in its **mantle cavity**, which is a hollow space inside the mantle. Water enters this space through a hole in the underside of the mantle, and the gills remove oxygen from the water. The muscles in the mantle then pump the water out through the **funnel tube**.

## Cirrate bodies

Many cirrate octopuses live in deep water. Their bodies have developed special features that help them survive in the cold, dark water.

*A pair of fins on the mantle are used for balance and swimming.*

*Some cirrate octopuses have protective shells, which grow inside their bodies.*

eye

webs

suckers

*Cirri on the arms of these octopuses help them find food.*

*An octopus has three hearts. Two hearts pump blood to the gills to collect oxygen. The third heart then pumps this blood throughout the octopus's body.*

## Get a move on!

An octopus can move very fast! It jets itself backward by forcing water out of its funnel tube. To change direction, it points its funnel tube a different way. As it moves, its arms trail behind. An octopus pulls its body along the ocean floor by using its suckers as suction cups.

11

# Sensing surroundings

Octopuses have excellent senses of sight, touch, taste, and smell. These senses have helped them survive in the ocean for millions of years. Octopuses adapt quickly to new environments by using the information they gather with their keen senses.

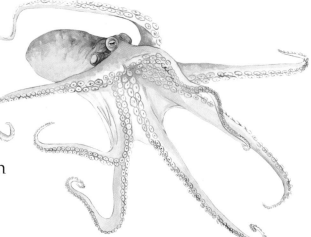

## Super suckers

An octopus's arms are lined with two rows of round suckers. Depending on its age and species, an octopus may have up to 240 suckers on each arm. It uses these sensitive suckers to touch, smell, and taste. Each sucker works independently. It has nerves attached to it that send messages to the octopus's brain. Without looking at an object, the octopus knows whether it is food—and can even tell if the food is tasty!

*Octopuses cannot hear. They rely on their other senses. Blind octopuses survive using just their suckers to gather information.*

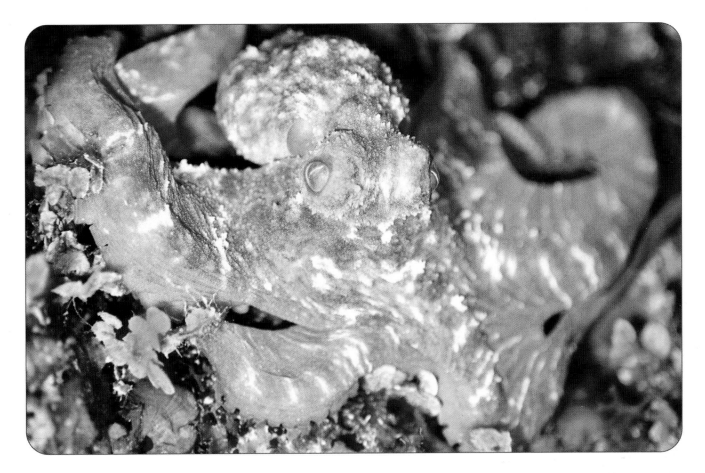

## Perfect vision

An octopus has very large eyes on either side of its mantle and can see sharp, clear images. Its brain knows what the octopus is looking at by identifying the size and shape of an object. Like most cephalopods, octopuses are probably **color-blind**, which means they see mostly in black and white.

## Pupil power

The **pupil** is the black part in the center of an eye. The pupils of an octopus (below) are always **horizontal**, or lined up with the ocean floor. No matter which way an octopus's body moves, its pupils stay horizontal, so the octopus knows which way is up or down. The pupils **dilate**, or increase in size, to allow in more light, giving the octopus good night vision. Being able to see in the dark helps an octopus hunt as well as watch out for **predators**.

The skin of an octopus is very loose. Short **connective tissues**, or fibers, attach the skin to the muscles underneath it. Different species of octopuses have different colored skin. The most common color is reddish brown, but octopuses are able to change the color of their skin to match their surroundings.

## Rainbow skin

An octopus's skin has tiny cells, called **chromatophores**, which are filled with colored chemicals. These cells receive messages from the octopus's brain. Each chromatophore reacts individually to these messages by expanding or contracting to change the color and pattern of the octopus's skin. Bright skin colors are created by fully expanded chromatophores. Pale skin colors are the result of contracted cells. Using tiny muscles, an octopus can also alter the **texture**, or feel, of the surface of its skin.

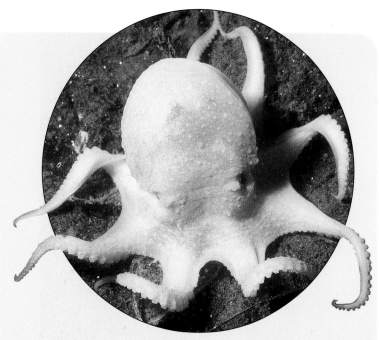

*Less than one second after sensing danger in its surroundings, this octopus changed the color of its skin from white (above) to red (below).*

14

# Blending in

An octopus changes both the color and the texture of its skin to **camouflage** itself, or blend in with its surroundings. When it is hiding in a coral reef (right), the octopus makes its skin multicolored and bumpy to resemble a piece of coral. When the animal is hiding on the sandy ocean floor (bottom), its skin turns brown and grainy to look just like sand. An octopus has **reflecting cells**, which respond to the amount of light in its surroundings. These cells may explain how octopuses are able to change their colors to match their environment so exactly, even though these animals are color-blind.

# Skin signals

An octopus also changes its skin to communicate with other animals. When an octopus is calm, its skin stays its normal color. When its skin changes to a deep red or dark brown, the animal is probably threatened or anxious. This color change is a signal to others to stay away! White or pale gray skin may mean the octopus is frightened or sick.

Many ocean animals, including moray eels, seals, sharks, and dolphins, eat octopuses. Octopuses depend on a variety of self-defense skills to hide and escape from these and other predators.

*Two-spot octopuses have circles on their skin that look like large eyes. These fake eyes may convince predators that the octopus is bigger than it really is.*

## Hide-and-seek

Octopuses are experts at hiding. Once they become aware of nearby predators, they hide under layers of sand or in crevices between rocks.

## Fake out

An octopus often camouflages itself by changing the color and texture of its skin. If it is discovered, it may try to make its body look bigger to scare a predator. To do so, the octopus spreads out its arms and puffs up its skin. It can also frighten a predator by raising the skin above its eyes to make itself look as if it has horns.

*Spiky skin and "horns" warn predators not to mess with this octopus!*

## Copy cat

One rare type of octopus is able to **mimic**, or imitate, other animals. The mimic octopus alters its shape, skin, and actions to look like another animal such as a sea snake or giant crab. It is not clear why this octopus mimics other animals, but this behavior is likely a way of fooling predators.

*mimic octopus*

## Ink stain

Most octopuses can shoot an inklike fluid through their funnel tubes. A threatened octopus aims a cloud of ink at its predator to create confusion. While the attacker is distracted by the dark cloud of ink, the octopus quickly jets away. The ink may also dull the predator's sense of smell, making it more difficult for it to locate the octopus. Some octopuses shoot ink in the shapes of their bodies. A predator may attack the ink **decoy**, or fake body, while the real octopus flees.

## Surprise!

If a predator grasps an octopus's arm, it may get a surprise. Some octopuses can detach their arms. While a predator is distracted by the detached arm, the octopus escapes. Octopuses can grow new arms to replace those that are lost. A new arm may have several tiny growths on its tip.

*The ink shooting out of this octopus's funnel tube forms a dark cloud streaming through the ocean.*

# Big brains

Octopuses are very intelligent compared to other mollusks. In fact, scientists believe that octopuses may be the most intelligent of all invertebrates. Octopuses have very large brains for invertebrates. They seem to be able to remember simple tasks and learn from experience. When placed in mazes, they appear to remember landmarks.

Even without landmarks, octopuses can remember their routes! In other tests, scientists sealed **prey** such as crabs in various containers. The octopuses learned how to open jars and bottles to reach the food. If one octopus watched another octopus get food out of a container, it was able to do the task much faster during its own turn.

*An octopus can get through a tiny opening—especially if there is a reward of food!*

## Gotcha!

Octopuses that live in tanks sometimes shoot streams of water at people standing close by—especially at the people who feed them. Researchers think this behavior is an octopus's way of getting attention—and food!

## Tank trouble

Octopuses that live in aquariums sometimes mimic the actions of other octopuses in nearby tanks. They also have been caught pushing open the lids of their aquariums and creeping out. Some hungry octopuses crawl into other tanks and eat their neighbors! Pet octopuses may attempt to escape from their aquariums by squeezing through the filter tubes or under the plastic floors of their homes.

## Funnel fun

The curiosity of octopuses is further proof that they are intelligent. Some octopuses appear to investigate and play with objects they find. Giant Pacific octopuses have been spotted bouncing pieces of trash back and forth, using jets of water from their funnel tubes.

*Divers report that octopuses appear to be interested in watching them. Octopuses are attracted to shiny objects such as camera lights.*

# Baby octopuses

Male and female octopuses of the same species **mate** in order to make babies. The female carries eggs inside her mantle. The eggs must have a male's **sperm** added to them for baby octopuses to start growing inside. A male mates with a female by putting his sperm into her mantle. He dies soon afterward. The female can store the sperm for up to ten months, until her eggs are ready to be fertilized. She may lay as few as 50 eggs or as many as 400,000 eggs, depending on her species. The pygmy octopus, for example, lays just a few large eggs, whereas the common octopus lays thousands of small eggs. The largest eggs are around one inch (25 mm) long. The smallest eggs are less than one-sixteenth of an inch (1.6 mm) long.

## Safety first

Octopus mothers search for safe dens in which to hide their eggs until they hatch. They use sticky **mucus** to string the eggs to the surfaces of the dens. Most octopuses stay near their eggs. Mothers may even stop hunting and eating so that they do not have to leave their dens.

## Mobile moms

In some species, mothers attach their eggs to the webs between their arms. They protect their eggs with their own bodies. The female tuberculate pelagic octopus is the only cephalopod that keeps fertilized eggs inside her body. Instead of laying the eggs, she gives birth to live octopuses.

## Short life spans

Most eggs laid in warm water hatch after a month. Eggs in cold water take longer to develop. Once the eggs hatch, the mother usually dies. The baby octopuses look like tiny adults. Most are eaten by predators, but those that live grow to full size quickly. Some species become adults, mate, and die in less than six months. Other species live up to five years.

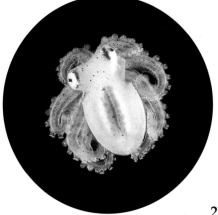

# Anything to eat?

Octopuses are **carnivores**, which means they eat other animals. They are also **scavengers** that eat **carrion**, or dead animals. Their most common foods include crabs, clams, lobsters, barnacles, shrimp, fish, and other cephalopods, including smaller octopuses. Most octopuses are **nocturnal**—they hunt and feed at night. They use their excellent night vision to locate prey. Hunting in darkness helps them hide from their prey. A few species, such as the Hawaiian day octopus, hunt in daylight. Prey animals may not notice this octopus approaching because it is so well camouflaged.

*Octopuses are among the most aggressive predators in the ocean. The octopus above has captured a fish to eat.*

## Mighty mouths

An octopus may collect a dozen or more prey animals before returning to its den to eat. It uses its hard beak to tear into the food. Its **radula**, or tongue, is covered with tiny teeth. The radula can drill a hole through even very hard shells. Some octopuses inject **toxin**, or poison, into the holes they drill. The toxin turns some animals into mush, which an octopus then scoops out with its tongue. Other prey are **paralyzed**, or lose their ability to move, by the toxin. They can no longer grip the inside of their shells, so they fall out. Octopuses also shoot their toxins at the eyes of prey.

*close-up of a mouth with beak in the center*

*close-up of the radula*

*A Caribbean reef octopus uses the webs between its arms to trap prey. It floats down through the water like a parachute, trapping its prey underneath it.*

## Sneak attack

An octopus may hide in its den until unsuspecting prey passes near the entrance. In a fast motion, it extends an arm out of the den and grabs the animal. Octopuses also crawl along the ocean floor, using their arms and suckers to find and capture bottom-dwelling prey. Cirrate octopuses use their cirri to find food and sweep it into their mouths.

23

# Ocean food web

To survive, every animal must eat plants or other animals. A **food chain** shows this pattern of eating and being eaten. A crab, for example, eats underwater plants, and an octopus eats the crab. The energy from the plant is passed on to the crab and then to the octopus.

Predators such as octopuses are near the top of a food chain. Predators that eat octopuses, such as sharks, are at the **apex**, or top, of a food chain. When an octopus eats animals from other food chains, the food chains connect to form a **food web**.

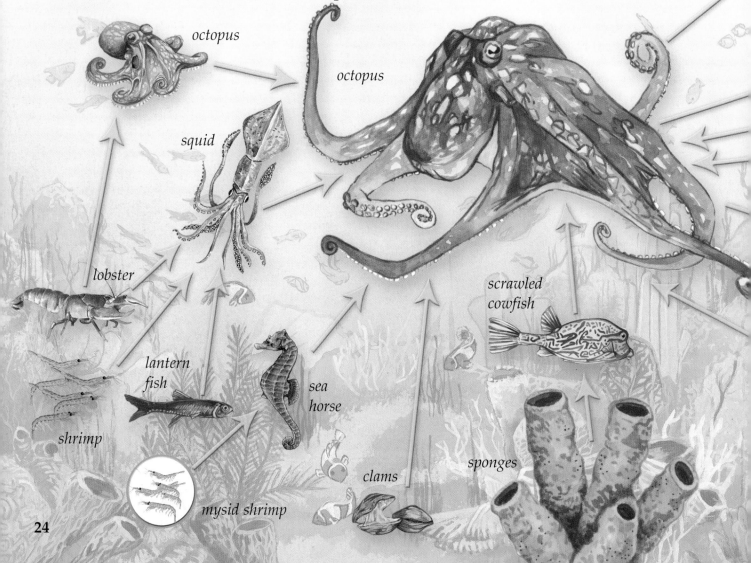

octopus

octopus

squid

lobster

scrawled cowfish

lantern fish

sea horse

shrimp

sponges

clams

mysid shrimp

24

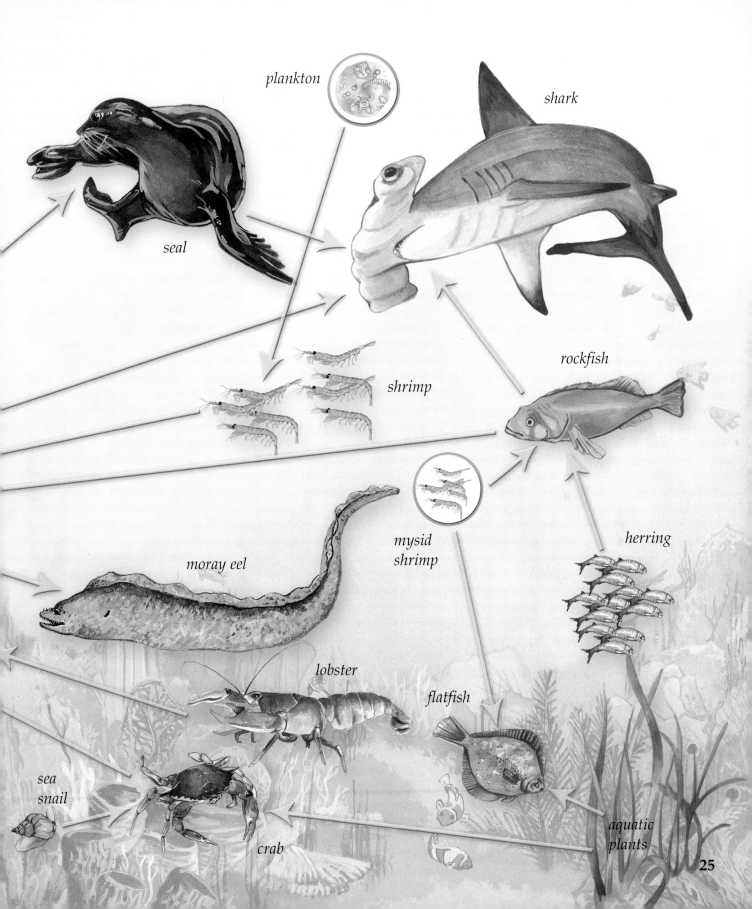

plankton

shark

seal

shrimp

rockfish

mysid
shrimp

herring

moray eel

lobster

flatfish

sea
snail

crab

aquatic
plants

Octopuses help balance the food webs to which they belong. This balance is very delicate. When links between food chains are broken, animals may starve. Threats such as **overfishing** lower the population of octopuses (see pages 30-31). When too many octopuses are fished from the ocean, there is not enough food available for predators such as moray eels and seals, and they starve.

## Going hungry

When there are fewer octopuses, fewer of their prey animals get eaten. The prey populations grow, but the amount of food available to them remains the same. There is not enough food for all the prey animals, which makes the food web unbalanced. Animals with overgrown populations quickly wipe out their food sources, and some of them may starve. The animals that hunt them then do not have enough food. Every part of the food web suffers. Even animals that are not part of an octopus's food chain are affected by the disappearance of octopuses because they are all connected to the same food web.

*When octopuses are in trouble, their predators and prey are also threatened. A damaged food web could wipe out all the plants and animals in a coral reef, such as that shown on the right.*

## Learn more!

Find out more about octopuses and marine life at these web sites:

- www.worldwildlife.org/oceans/oceans.cfm
- http://natzoo.si.edu/animals/oceanliving
- www.ocean.com/conservation

# Octopuses and people

In the past, people told stories of octopuses wrapping their arms around sailors and swimmers and squeezing them to death. Researchers have proven these tales to be false. In fact, they report that octopuses are shy. When faced with a threat, these animals will retreat rather than fight. They attack only as a last resort. Octopuses are very curious, however, and are attracted to bright objects. Some try to grab shiny items such as divers' jewelry!

## Stop, thief!

Fishers in some areas consider octopuses to be pests. Octopuses often squeeze into small spaces, such as crab and lobster traps, and feast on the catch. When they are finished eating, they slip back out of the traps. Sometimes fishers have nothing to show for their work because of these sneaky cephalopods! In fact, octopuses cost fishers millions of dollars each year.

## Small but deadly

The blue-ringed octopus, shown right, is only the size of a golf ball, but it can seriously injure a person. Victims that come into contact with this octopus's poison are paralyzed and unable to breathe. Only a few people have died after being poisoned, however. The blue-ringed octopus does not seek to harm people. When it poisons someone, it is usually because a person mishandled this animal.

*The patterns on the body of the blue-ringed octopus turn bright blue when this octopus is threatened.*

## Not your average pet

Octopuses are very interesting, but they are not suited to living in captivity. Many, however, are kept in public and private aquariums. Some are shipped around the world to new owners, but very few survive the stress of a long trip. Octopuses also have much shorter life spans than some other pets. A mature octopus may live only a month or two after it is purchased. Octopuses that live in tanks spend much of their time hiding. Nocturnal species may appear only in the middle of the night when they are in search of food.

*Octopuses are not meant to be pets. To survive, they need to live in their natural habitats.*

# Dangers to octopuses

People may be the biggest threat to the survival of octopuses. Octopus fishing is a multimillion dollar industry. Fishers use nets, spears, or fake dens made of wooden crates to catch octopuses. Some fishers also squirt chlorine bleach into octopus dens to irritate octopuses, which then swim out into the nets covering their dens. Some fishing boats operate as floating factories. The people on these boats overfish octopuses without any concern for the damage they do to the ocean and its food webs. Sometimes fishers set traps for fish and other animals and catch octopuses by accident. Octopuses snared as **bycatch** are often thrown away.

*Well over 100,000 tons of octopuses are fished and sold to restaurants every year.*

## Disaster area

Pollution and environmental disasters such as oil spills are very hazardous to octopuses. Damage to the ocean environment can ruin octopus habitats and kill many prey animals, leaving octopuses with less food. In some cases, the pollution in the water is enough to kill a local octopus population.

## Endangered?

There is not enough information on octopus populations to know if they are shrinking, so it is difficult to know whether any species is **endangered**. A species may be disappearing before people discover it exists. Only about five percent of octopus species have been studied. Some may disappear before people learn anything about them.

*This oil spill covered an entire coastline. The plants and animals that once thrived there lost their habitats, food sources—and lives!*

## Respecting the ocean

As the number of swimmers, snorkelers, and divers in the oceans increases, so does the amount of water pollution and trash being left in the water. This increased "traffic" may destroy some octopus habitats. Many divers wear gloves to protect their hands. When they touch octopuses, their rough gloves often tear the animals' skin.

# Glossary

Note: Boldfaced words that are defined in the book may not appear in the glossary.

**adapt** To change over time in order to become better suited to an environment

**bioluminescent** Describing an animal's ability to produce its own light

**bycatch** An animal that is accidentally caught in a net intended for another animal

**cephalopod** A type of underwater mollusk

**cirrate** Describing a subgroup of octopus species that have fins, large webs, and cirri

**cirri** Hairlike growths on the arms of some octopus species

**endangered** Describing a living thing that is in danger of becoming extinct

**gill** An organ that fish and some other aquatic animals use to remove oxygen from water

**habitat** The natural place where an animal lives

**incirrate** Describing a subgroup of octopus species that does not have cirri

**mate** To come together to make babies

**mucus** A moist, sticky substance produced by some animals

**overfish** To take so many of one marine species from an area that the species becomes threatened

**predator** An animal that hunts and eats other animals

**prey** An animal that is hunted and eaten by another animal

**scavenger** An animal that feeds on the flesh of dead animals instead of hunting

**sperm** A male cell that joins with a female's egg to produce a baby

**tentacle** A long, flexible body part an invertebrate uses for feeling, grasping, and moving

# Index

1 2 3 4 5 6 7 8 9 0   Printed in the U.S.A.   2 1 0 9 8 7 6 5 4 3